Adventurous

SAINTS
AROUND THE WORLD

Meg Hunter-Kilmer

Illustrated by Lindsey Sanders

Bl. Peter Kasui Kibe

Peter KAH-soo-ee KEE-beh

 Peter never, never, never gave up. He wanted to do God's will, no matter the cost. When people tried to stop him from becoming a priest, Peter just kept trying. He went to China and India and finally to Rome, traveling halfway around the world and back again. It took him years and years and years, but Father Peter finally made it back to Japan to serve his people as a priest.

Bl. Peter teaches us never to give up, no matter what.

Japan

1587–1639

Feast Day: July 1

St. Dulce Pontes

DOOL-see POHN-cheess

Dulce didn't have plans to change the world. No, she just wanted to help whoever was in front of her. But all her good deeds began to add up. They made her so brave that once she broke open the window of a crashed bus to pull people to safety before the bus burst into flames! Sister Dulce's faithfulness in small things built her up into a hero who changed the world.

St. Dulce teaches us to serve well in small things and trust that God will do the rest.

Brazil

1914–1992

Feast Day: August 13

Bl. Emilian Kovch

Emilian never abandoned anyone, no matter what it cost him—even when wicked men forced Jewish people into a building and set it on fire. Father Emilian came running to stop them, then went into the burning building to bring people out to safety. He loved people so much that when he was sent to prison, he asked to stay so that he could hear the prisoners' confessions—because he wouldn't leave anyone behind.

Bl. Emilian teaches us to be courageous and help others.

Ukraine, Poland

1884–1944

Feast Day: March 25

St. Damien of Molokai

DAY-mee-uhn of MOLE-oh-kie
(more accurately, MOLE-oh-kah-EE)

 Damien was an awfully hard worker. When he became a priest in Hawaii, he needed all of his strength to climb the giant mountains to get to his people. He needed it even more when he moved to a small island where people lived with the terrible disease of leprosy. He worked hard to show them God's love. Even when he got leprosy, he never stopped loving them and loving God.

St. Damien teaches us to work hard to serve God and his people.

Belgium, United States

1840–1889

Feast Day: May 10

St. María Antonia de Paz y Figueroa

ma-REE-a ahn-TONE-ya deh PAHSS ee FEE-gay-ROE-ah | Mama Antula: MAH-mah ahn-TOO-lah

Did you know that sometimes to be obedient to God you have to be a rebel? St. Mama Antula was a rebel, though she never set out to be. She just wanted to help people learn to pray, so she walked all around Argentina—barefoot. Lots of people said she was crazy or even wicked, but Mama Antula didn't care what they thought, and soon they all knew that she was a strong and holy rebel.

St. Mama Antula teaches us not to worry about what other people think.

Argentina

1730–1799

Feast Day: March 7

St. Laura Montoya

Laura mon-TOY-ah

 **E**veryone thought St. Laura was crazy for going into the jungle to serve Indigenous people. They made fun of her and tried to stop her and warned her that she wouldn't be safe. But she didn't care. She knew what it was like to feel unloved, and she wanted to make sure nobody else felt that way. So off she went into the jungle to love the people everybody else ignored.

St. Laura teaches us to look out for people who are treated badly.

Colombia

1874–1949

Feast Day: October 21

St. Joseph Vaz

Joseph VAHZ

When St. Joseph heard about people who hadn't seen priests for thirty years, he knew he had to help them. So Father Joseph put on a disguise (with the things he needed for Mass tied around his waist) and slipped into Sri Lanka. He had to stay undercover, so he wore a rosary around his neck to signal to people that he was a priest. Then he snuck all around celebrating sacraments for people!

St. Joseph teaches us never to give up when people need our help.

India, Sri Lanka

1651–1711

Feast Day: January 16

Bl. Ladislaus Bukowinski

LOD-iss-LOSS BOO-ko-VEENG-skee

Ladislaus had been put in prison for no good reason. When wicked men began shooting into a crowd of prisoners, he crawled around giving wounded people absolution. Later he was sent to a country where it was illegal to celebrate Mass, but he traveled all around to bring the sacraments in secret to people who risked their lives to receive them. None of it was fair, but God brought good out of it all.

Bl. Ladislaus teaches us that God is directing our lives, even when it doesn't look that way.

Poland, Kazakhstan

1904–1974

Feast Day: June 20

Bl. Sara Salkaházi

Sara SHAHL-ka-HAH-zee *(ka as in cat)*

Sara never quite fit in. Even her Sisters weren't sure if they wanted her. But Sister Sara knew God was calling her to be a Sister, and she knew he was calling her to be just the way he made her. So she used her gifts to publish a magazine and start a college and serve the poor—and save hundreds of Jewish people's lives. Sister Sara was a gift exactly the way she was.

Bl. Sara teaches us to trust that God made us good, just as we are.

Slovakia, Hungary

1899–1944

Feast Day: December 27

Bl. Victoire Rasoamanarivo

vic-TWAHR rah-SOO-ah-mah-nah-REE-voo

When soldiers stood at the church door to threaten anyone who wanted to enter, Bl. Victoire walked right up and said, "If you must have blood, start with mine." She was awfully brave! But she was also clever; she was the queen's cousin and was pretty sure she could keep her people safe. She used all her power and all her wisdom to lead the Catholics of Madagascar for three years.

Bl. Victoire teaches us to be brave as well as clever when we serve God.

Madagascar

1848–1894

Feast Day: August 21

St. Barnabas

BAR-na-bus

Barnabas traveled all around, preaching the Gospel to thousands of people—all because he trusted in the power of God. When St. Paul said that he had met Jesus, nobody believed him. Paul had persecuted them, so people were suspicious and afraid. But Barnabas knew how powerful God is. So he took a risk: he went to talk to Paul. And after that his whole life was a grand adventure.

St. Barnabas teaches us to love people without holding anything back.

Cyprus

d. 61

Feast Day: June 11

Bl. Maria Therese von Wüllenweber

ma-REE-ah tuh-RAY-suh fon VOO-len-VEB-er

Bl. Maria Therese had no idea what she was supposed to do with her life. Or, rather, she had many ideas, and every one of them ended up being wrong. She entered one religious order after another and left one religious order after another. It wasn't until she was fifty-five that she finally found her calling! But she knew that God had always been working and had never stopped leading her.

Bl. Maria Therese teaches us that God knows what he's doing even when we don't.

Germany, Italy

1833–1907

Feast Day: December 25

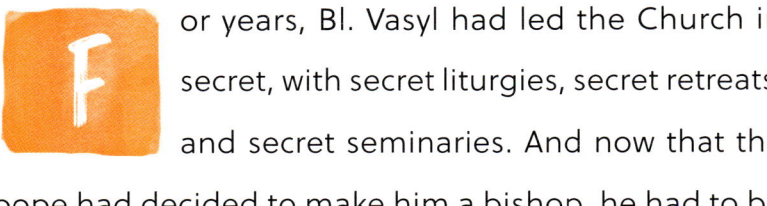

Bl. Vasyl Velychkovsky

vah-SIL VEL-ish-KOHF-skee

or years, Bl. Vasyl had led the Church in secret, with secret liturgies, secret retreats, and secret seminaries. And now that the pope had decided to make him a bishop, he had to be consecrated in a secret hotel room ceremony. It wasn't what he'd imagined, but he was just glad to be able to serve God and his Church—and glad to be reminded that God will never abandon his people.

Bl. Vasyl teaches us that God is always taking care of us.

Ukraine, Canada

1903–1973

Feast Day: June 30

Bl. Peter To Rot

Peter TOE ROTE

hen soldiers told Bl. Peter and his people that they weren't allowed to go to Mass anymore, Peter built a chapel in the woods so they could pray in secret. He helped to hide a priest, then brought the Eucharist from the priest's hiding place so that people could receive Communion. He'd never expected to be an undercover leader in the Church, just a regular husband and dad, but God's plans are always surprising.

Bl. Peter teaches us that God can do big things with us when we say yes to him in small things.

Papua New Guinea

1912–1945

Feast Day: July 7

St. Rafael Guízar y Valencia

rahf-ah-YEL GHEE-sar ee bah-LEN-see-ah

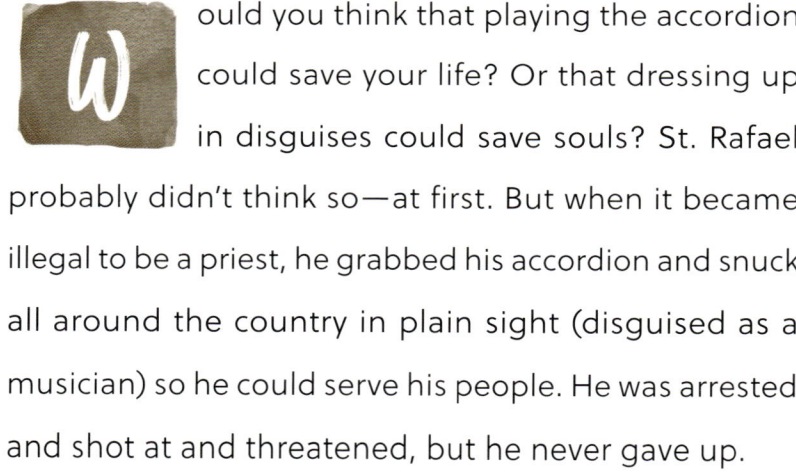

ould you think that playing the accordion could save your life? Or that dressing up in disguises could save souls? St. Rafael probably didn't think so—at first. But when it became illegal to be a priest, he grabbed his accordion and snuck all around the country in plain sight (disguised as a musician) so he could serve his people. He was arrested and shot at and threatened, but he never gave up.

St. Rafael teaches us to be brave when serving God becomes hard.

Mexico

1878–1938

Feast Day: June 6